MY FRIEND has Epilepsy

BY ANNA LEVENE

Chrysalis Education

Distributed in the United States by
Smart Apple Media
1980 Lookout Drive
North Mankato, MN 56003

Copyright © Chrysalis Books PLC 2003

ISBN 1-93233-328-2
Library of Congress Control Number 2003102563

Editorial Manager: Joyce Bentley
Senior Editor: Sarah Nunn
Project Editor: Sue Nicholson
Designer: Wladek Szechter
Photographer: Michael Wicks
Picture Researcher: Terry Forshaw
Illustrations: Tom Connell

Consultants: Kathy Bairstow and John Stormont, Epilepsy Action
Epilepsy Action is a U.K. charity that aims to improve the quality of life and promote the interests of people living with epilepsy.

The photographer and publishers would like to thank David Hammond; Billy, Jane and Joe McHale; Pam, Rebecca and Sophie Ryan; Vanessa Tobie; and the Pinn Medical Centre for their help in preparing this book.

Picture acknowledgements:
19 (top), Science Photo Library; 19 (bottom), Mehau Kulyk/Science Photo Library; 21 (bottom), Geray Sweeney/Corbis; 29 (bottom), Candice Farmer/Getty Images

Printed in Hong Kong

10 9 8 7 6 5 4 3 2 1

Contents

*Words in **bold** are explained in the glossary on page 30.*

My friend Grace

Grace developed epilepsy a year ago.

Hello! I'm Jodie and this is my friend Grace. We've been best friends since we started going to dance class together. We're both crazy about modern dance. At the end of term we're performing in the school play.

About a year ago, it looked like Grace might have to give up dancing. She suddenly started passing out. The first time it happened she thought she'd just

Now Grace's epilepsy is under control, she has lots of energy for dancing.

Dr. Mitchell is a neurologist. He gave Grace medicine to control her epilepsy.

fainted. But then she collapsed again, so her mom took her to the doctor. The doctor asked lots of questions and then said Grace would have to see another type of doctor, called a **neurologist**.

This doctor, Dr. Mitchell, did some tests on Grace. The results showed that she had **epilepsy**. He gave Grace special medicine to take, but it made her feel sleepy all the time so he changed it. The next medicine made Grace feel sick. Finally, Dr. Mitchell found another medicine that didn't make Grace feel sleepy or sick.

It was really good to go to dance class together again!

EPILEPSY FACTS

CHILDREN WITH EPILEPSY

Over two million people in the U.S. have epilepsy, and that includes about 316,000 children under age 14. Nearly half of all people with epilepsy develop it by the age of eleven. Most types of epilepsy can be kept under control with medicine.

Finding out about epilepsy

When Dr. Mitchell told Grace that she had epilepsy, she didn't know what it was. So Dr Mitchell explained. He said,

"Most of the time you are in control of your body. For example, if you decide you want to draw a picture, your **brain** sends a message to your fingers to pick up a pencil. The message travels so quickly you don't know it's been sent. But if you have epilepsy, messages from your brain get mixed up. Then, depending on what type of epilepsy you have, you may pass out or start behaving in a strange way. This is called having a **seizure**."

Dr. Mitchell told Grace that seizures are not usually dangerous but because they come without warning, people can hurt themselves while they are having one. He said that some people with epilepsy know they're going to have a seizure because they feel strange or notice a funny smell. This is called an **aura**. They can then sit or lie in a safe place before their seizure starts.

People with epilepsy look and behave just like anyone else. Unless they have a seizure, no one can tell they have epilepsy.

Opposite: **Grace sleeps for a long time as part of her seizure.**

This girl is having a kind of seizure called an absence.

EPILEPSY FACTS

KINDS OF SEIZURE

One kind of seizure is called an **absence**, or petit mal, in which the person stares into space for a few seconds or minutes. Grace's type of seizure is called a **tonic-clonic seizure**, or grand mal. In this type of seizure the person may fall to the ground, start twitching, and (when the seizure is over) sleep deeply for a long time. Most people do not remember what has happened after a seizure.

What causes seizures?

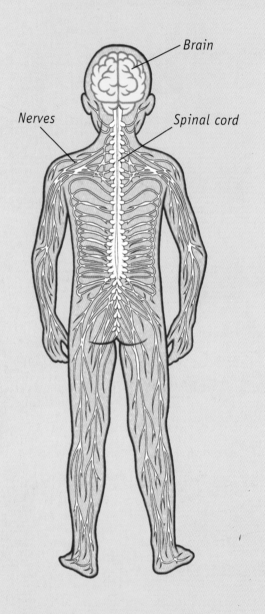

Brain

Nerves

Spinal cord

A network of nerves connects the brain and spinal cord to every part of your body.

Epileptic seizures start in the brain. Your brain controls how your body works by sending and receiving electrical signals to and from different parts of the body. The signals act as messages, telling the body what to do. The signals travel along bundles of fine hair-like threads called **nerves**. Together the brain, **spinal cord**, and nerves form the **nervous system**.

The signals that run from your brain to different parts of your body can be reflex or voluntary. If dust gets up your nose, you sneeze, without thinking about it. This is a reflex signal. If you want to ride a bicycle, your brain sends signals to your legs to push the pedals round. These are voluntary signals.

Usually, the body's message system works really well, but if someone has epilepsy, the brain can get over-excited. It sends so many signals that they get confused and the body doesn't know which messages to obey. The result is a seizure.

The type of seizure a person has depends on which part of the brain—and how much of it—is affected. Different parts of the brain control different parts of the body. For example, Most of the muscles that move your head, **torso**, legs, and arms are controlled by an area running across the middle of your brain called the **motor cortex**.

If the motor cortex sends out too many messages too quickly, a seizure will start with twitching movements in one of these areas, such as the face, a hand, a leg, or a foot.

The motor cortex (colored in purple) controls movement. Other parts of your brain control different things.

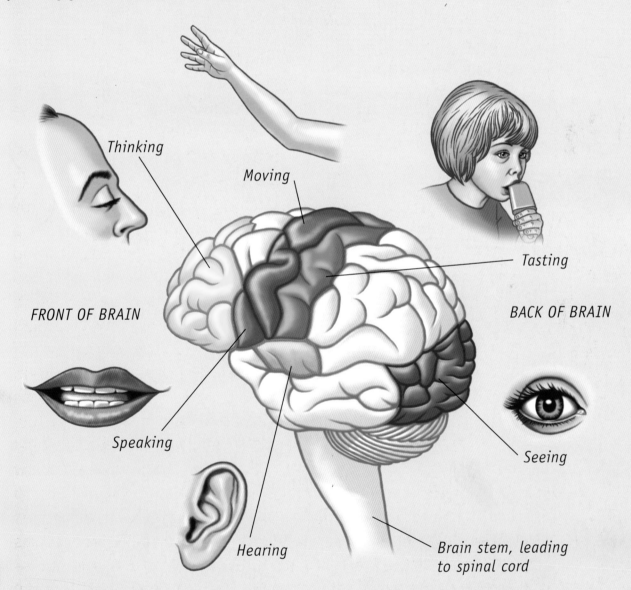

Thinking

Moving

Tasting

FRONT OF BRAIN

BACK OF BRAIN

Speaking

Seeing

Hearing

Brain stem, leading to spinal cord

At school

On schooldays, I get to Grace's house at a quarter after eight. Sometimes, I'm a bit early and have to wait until Grace has finished her breakfast and swallowed her tablets. She has to take two tablets in the morning and another two twelve hours later. The tablets help stop Grace having a seizure. She has to take them at the same time every day.

Before Dr. Mitchell found a medicine that suited her, Grace was often away from school. She felt ill and was scared she might have a seizure in class. When she did come to school, she couldn't concentrate. She began to get bad marks, even though she'd always been near the top of the class. Some of the other children began to tease Grace. She felt really miserable.

"Why do I have to have epilepsy?" she used to say. "It's not fair!"

Now Grace is much happier. She's caught up with all the work she missed and she doesn't worry about having a seizure. Even if she does, her mom has told the teachers what to expect and she knows that they will look after her.

Opposite: **Grace takes two tablets twice every day to control her epilepsy. Now she hardly ever has a seizure.**

Once Grace's epilepsy was under control, she soon started to do well again at school.

EPILEPSY FACTS

CONTROLLING EPILEPSY

Most people develop epilepsy when they are children. They are usually neither more nor less clever than anyone else. But until their epilepsy is fully under control, children like Grace may miss a lot of school. They may fall behind with their schoolwork and do less well in class. They can soon lose confidence. So it's important that their epilepsy is brought quickly under control.

Our favorite lessons

Grace is good at English while I'm better at science, but the lessons we both like best are with computers. We also take turns using the laptop Grace's mom has at home. It's really fun working on that. It's annoying when my little sister Sophie's with me because she then wants to have a go too!

When Grace's mom first told the school that Grace had epilepsy, our teacher said Grace couldn't use the computer any more. He thought the flickering from the screen would cause a seizure. Grace was really upset so her mom went to see the Principal, Mrs Peters, to explain that Grace wasn't affected by TV or computer screens. She brought Mrs. Peters an information pack about epilepsy for all the teachers.

At first, the swimming teacher wasn't sure Grace should have swimming lessons in case she had a seizure in the pool. But once he knew that Grace's epilepsy was under control, he allowed Grace to swim again and organized the class so that everyone swam in pairs. Then if Grace did have a seizure, her partner could call for help.

Opposite: **Grace's mom explained to the Principal that Grace's epilepsy is under control. This means that, with care, Grace can do everything other children can do at school.**

Grace and her mom enjoy watching television together. It is good to know that the flickering of the screen will not cause Grace to have a seizure.

EPILEPSY FACTS

SCREENS AND SEIZURES

Many people think that the flickering from TV and computer screens is a common cause of epileptic seizures. In fact, only about 4 in every 100 people with epilepsy are affected by it. However, if a seizure is caused by flickering from a screen, it is sensible to watch television from a distance of at least 6 ft 6 in. in a well-lit room and to use a remote control to change channels.

Most people with epilepsy are not troubled by a flickering computer screen.

At Grace's house

After school, I sometimes go to Grace's house and stay for supper. Her mom always makes us something really tasty. Her pot roast is the best!

Dr. Mitchell told Grace it is especially important for her to keep fit and healthy. Lack of sleep and missed meals often cause seizures. He said she should take some exercise every day, and make sure she ate a healthy diet.

"Cut down on takeout foods and meals from a packet or jar, and eat lots of fruit and vegetables," he said. "At least five servings a day."

At first Grace didn't like the sound of that at all.

"What am I going to eat?" she wailed.

But Grace's mom is a good cook, and she knows how to make meals that Grace likes. I like them, too—and healthy meals are good for our dancing!

Dr. Mitchell also said Grace shouldn't rush or skip a meal. So now she gets up fifteen minutes earlier to finish her cereal and toast and goes to bed a little earlier, too.

After supper, we usually go to Grace's room. She used to have a raised platform bed but now she's got a wide, low bed which her mom says is safer. It's great for somersaults!

Grace also has a lovely new soft carpet. She chose it herself. Even when you roll off the bed, it doesn't hurt.

Grace has a low bed and soft carpet to help keep her safe in her bedroom.

Opposite: **Grace and Jodie know that eating fruit helps to keep them fit and healthy.**

Keeping safe

Grace sometimes gets fed up because she feels her mum won't let her do as much as other children her age. For a few weeks after she was **diagnosed**, Grace's mum was scared to allow Grace anywhere on her own. Even when Grace went to the lavatory, her mum would wait outside!

Now her mum's a bit more relaxed. Grace's tablets are working well and she hasn't had a seizure for months.

Even so, Grace's mum doesn't like her going anywhere on her own – even down the road to my house.

"What would happen if you had a seizure?" she asks. "A passer-by probably wouldn't know what to do. People might not even stop to help you."

Although Grace's mum worries about Grace, she does let her come out with me and other friends. We often go cycling round the park.

Next term our class is going on a school trip to France. Grace spent ages persuading her mum to let her go.

"Pleeeease!" she begged. "If you don't say yes, I'll be the only one not going."

Finally her mum agreed. She didn't want Grace to feel left out.

"Just remember to take your tablets on time, and to eat sensibly," she said.

Grace shows her mum the brochure for her class's trip to France.

Opposite: **Grace and Jodie like riding in the park. It's more fun, and safer, when they're together.**

EPILEPSY FACTS

WEARING ID

People with epilepsy sometimes wear a special ID (identity) bracelet or necklace engraved with their name and address and information about their condition. It may also give an emergency telephone number, which people can phone if they need advice on how to help someone who is having a seizure.

Grave wears a special necklace engraved with information about her epilepsy.

Diagnosing epilepsy

Grace's mom called the doctor while Grace recovered from her seizure.

Grace doesn't talk about her epilepsy much. So one day I asked her mom how Dr. Mitchell knew for sure that Grace had epilepsy. She said:

"When Grace passed out for the second time, I knew she hadn't fainted. She was lying on the floor and breathing unevenly. Then her legs and arms began to twitch. It was frightening to watch because I didn't know what was wrong with her. After a minute or two she lay still and fell into a deep sleep, so I picked her up and put her on the sofa. She slept for a long time. When she woke up she didn't know what had happened. She was confused and a bit weepy.

"We took Grace to Dr. Mitchell, a neurologist. He asked us all sorts of questions then said he wanted Grace to have an **EEG**, to record the pattern made by electrical signals in Grace's brain.

"Grace lay on a couch while a nurse stuck pads all over her head. The pads had wires attached to them which fed into a machine. Then Grace had to lie still for a half hour. From time to time, the nurse asked her to breathe deeply, or open and close her eyes. Once or twice she flashed a strong light into Grace's eyes.

"Meanwhile, the machine rolled out a long piece of paper with spiky lines on it. Dr. Mitchell said the pattern made by the lines showed that Grace almost certainly had epilepsy."

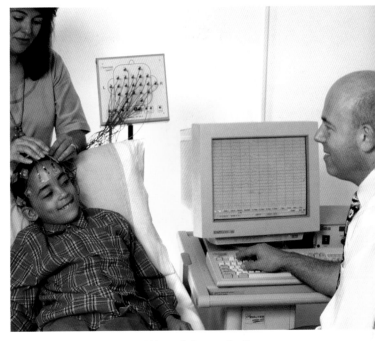

Grace had an EEG like this to help diagnose her epilepsy.

Another type of scan to see why a person has epilepsy is called an MRI scan. This photograph shows an MRI scan of a healthy brain.

EPILEPSY FACTS

CT SCANS

One way of finding out why someone has epilepsy is to do a **CT scan**. A kind of camera called a scanner takes X-ray pictures of a person's brain. The pictures are fed into a computer, which transfers them onto a screen. The doctor checks the pictures to see if any parts of the brain have been damaged in a way that causes epilepsy.

Who gets epilepsy?

People who come from families with a history of epilepsy are more likely to develop epilepsy themselves.

Right: **Grace knows she's going to have a seizure when everything looks blurred and sounds a long way away.**

Anyone can get epilepsy, but most people develop it before the age of twenty.

People may develop seizures because of infection or illness, such as meningitis, as a result of a serious head injury, or because part of their brain has been damaged during birth. Some people are more likely to develop epilepsy because they come from families with a history of epilepsy. However, for most people there is no obvious cause.

Although some people have epilepsy from birth, it is difficult to diagnose young babies. Seizures in older children are easier to recognize. Some children can describe how they felt before, during, and after a seizure. Others may have an aura. They may feel restless, their skin might tingle, or they might see flashes of light.

Anything which causes a seizure is called a **trigger**. Once people have had several seizures they can begin to work out what triggers them. They may not be getting enough sleep, they may have missed a meal, or they may be ill. A few people react badly to flickering television or computer screens, or to strobe lights. When people know what triggers their seizures, they can try to avoid them.

It is rare for strobe lights to cause a seizure. People who have epilepsy can find out if they are sensitive to flashing lights from the results of an EEG.

Having a sleepover

Grace and I used to stay with each other a lot. But when Grace found out she had epilepsy, she stopped coming for a while. Grace's mom was worried about her being away from home, and Grace was afraid she might have a seizure at our house. She told me later that she dribbles and sometimes wets herself during a seizure.

But when Grace started feeling better, we both thought it would be fun if she came for a sleepover again. My mom and dad were a bit nervous, but Grace's mom told them not to worry. All they had to do was make sure that Grace took her tablets on time, didn't eat supper too late, and slept for at least eight hours.

"If Grace says she feels odd, just 'phone and I'll come round straightaway," she said.

Nothing went wrong and now Grace spends almost every Saturday night at my house. We have a great time. My mom always gives us something really nice to eat and when we go to bed, I pull my mattress off my bed and we sleep on the floor. Usually she makes us go upstairs quite early—but if there's a good television program on, she lets us stay up a bit later. She makes sure we don't get woken up too early the next morning.

Grace usually has to go to bed quite early, but on Saturday nights she's allowed to stay up a bit later.

Opposite: **Jodie's mom often makes pizza because she knows both girls like it. Although it's important for Grace to eat regular, well-balanced meals, she is allowed treats from time to time.**

Having a check-up

Every few months Grace goes see Dr. Mitchell to make sure her tablets are controlling her epilepsy properly. Grace says:

"Dr. Mitchell asks me how I'm feeling, and whether I've had any seizures since I last saw him. He may give me a blood test to check I'm taking the right amount of medicine and that it's still the best type of medicine for my sort of epilepsy. He's told me that as I get bigger, we may have to increase the **dose**.

"He then asks to see my record card. My mom usually fills it in. If I have a seizure, she writes down exactly what happened. She asks what I was feeling or thinking immediately before it started, and what I remember about it afterwards. Often I don't remember very much.

"Dr. Mitchell says it's important the record card is filled in as accurately as possible. That way we can work out what triggers my seizures and then I can try to avoid those triggers. So far, we know that being very tired or hungry makes it more likely I'll have a seizure. That's why mom fusses about what I eat and when I go to bed.

"Sometimes I get fed up about having to be so careful, although Dr. Mitchell says there's a good chance I'll grow out of my epilepsy before I reach my twenties. But even if I don't, now my epilepsy's under control, it doesn't really bother me most of the time."

Grace's mom fills in Grace's record card.

Opposite: **Grace has regular check-ups to make sure her tablets are still controlling her epilepsy.**

EPILEPSY FACTS

GROWING OUT OF EPILEPSY

Many children with epilepsy grow out of it by the time they are adults. Others have to go on taking medication throughout their lives. A few are able to have an operation to stop them having seizures, but only children with certain types of epilepsy are suitable for this.

Best friends

Before Grace's epilepsy was under control, when she felt tired and ill all the time, I was scared that we wouldn't stay friends. She seemed to have changed so much. I think Grace was scared, too. She had to stay off school a lot, and when she was there, she'd hardly talk. At weekends she just wanted to stay at home.

Now Grace is used to having epilepsy and taking her medicine, and she feels more in control. She knows that if she takes her tablets on time and stays healthy, she can do almost everything her friends do.

"If I'm lucky, I may grow out of my epilepsy," she says. "And if I don't then it won't matter too much. There are still lots of jobs I can do—like working with computers, or becoming a dancer!"

As for me, I'm just glad Grace is happy and well again, and that we're still best friends.

Best friends Grace and Jodie can't wait for the first performance of their school show.

*Opposite: **Grace can do almost anything her friends can do and hardly thinks about her epilepsy at all.***

EPILEPSY FACTS

WORLD OF WORK

There are only a few jobs that people with epilepsy are not likely to do. For example, epileptics are not likely to join the uniformed services (such as the army, police, or fire department), or become a truck driver, pilot, or deep-sea diver. However, more jobs are opening up as epilepsy becomes better understood and treatment for it improves.

Questions people ask

Q. **What should I do if someone has a seizure?**

A. If someone has a seizure:

- Stay with the person while someone finds an adult.
- Remove any sharp or hard objects nearby.
- If they have fallen, put something soft under their head.

- When the seizure is over, tilt their head back and make sure nothing is blocking their airways. Try to roll them onto their side.
- Stay with them until they have recovered.

DO NOT try to move them or put anything in their mouth.

Stay with someone who is having a seizure until the seizure is over.

Q. **Do children with epilepsy find it harder to learn?**

A. Most children with epilepsy have the same range of intelligence and abilities as those without epilepsy. However, a few children with epilepsy do find it harder to learn. This may be because their epilepsy is affecting the part of the brain that deals with memory. It could be that they are missing a lot of school. Or, it may simply be that their medicine is causing problems, in which case the dose or type of medicine will almost certainly be changed.

Q. **Do animals have epilepsy?**

A. Yes. Any animal with a brain can have epileptic seizures. Cats often have seizures in their sleep. Epilepsy in both dogs and cats is increasing. Like humans, seizures in animals can be controlled with medicine.

Q. **Can you drive if you have epilepsy?**
A. Epileptics may drive if seizures are controlled. How long you must be seizure-free varies. It is usually from three months to a year. Many epileptics do not drive.

If you have epilepsy you may only be able to drive if you have not had a seizure for at least a year.

People with epilepsy can do most sports, such as swimming.

Q. **Have there been any famous people with epilepsy?**
A. Yes, lots. For example, the soldiers and statesmen Julius Caesar and Napoleon Bonaparte, the composer Pyotr Tchaikovsky, the artist Vincent van Gogh, and the writer Ernest Hemingway.

Q. **Are there any sports people can't do if they have epilepsy?**
A. People with epilepsy can usually do most sports, although special care should be taken with some. Anyone who goes bicycling, or rides horses, for example, should always wear a helmet—but this is particularly important for someone with epilepsy in case they have a seizure and fall. Swimmers or climbers should always go with someone else. For safety reasons, people with epilepsy are not encouraged to go solo parachuting, scuba diving, or motor racing.

Glossary

absence A type of seizure in which the person stares into space and looks at if he or she is daydreaming. An absence is sometimes called a "petit mal", which is French for "little illness."

aura A warning that someone may get when a seizure is about to start.

brain An organ in the head that controls everything we do by receiving and sending messages to different parts of our bodies along our nerves.

CT scan A type of scan or picture made when X-rays are passed through the body, producing an image of the inside of the body on a computer screen. [CT stands for computed tomography.]

diagnose To identify a disease by its symptoms.

dose A measured amount of medicine.

EEG (electroencephalogram) A test that records electrical messages sent out by the brain.

epilepsy A condition of the nervous system which can result in a seizure. The word epilepsy comes from the Ancient Greek language. It means "to take hold of," or "seize."

grand mal *see* **tonic-clonic seizure**

motor cortex Part of the brain that controls movement.

MRI scan A type of scan or picture of the body in which a strong magnet picks up signals from a person's brain. The signals are fed into a computer and a picture of the brain appears on a screen. [MRI stands for Magnetic Resonance Image.]

nerves Bundles of fibers that pass messages through the body to and from the brain. They form a network that links every part of your body with your brain.

nervous system A network of nerves running through the body, controlled by the brain.

neurologist A doctor who specializes in the diagnosis and treatment of the body's nervous system.

petit mal *see* **absence**

seizure What may happen when messages sent to the brain get confused. A person having a seizure may stare into space or fall to the ground and twitch. A seizure usually lasts from a few seconds to a few minutes. (*see* **absence** and **tonic-clonic seizure**)

spinal cord A thick bundle of nerves running down the middle of your back. It receives messages from your nerves and carries them up to your brain.

tonic-clonic seizure A type of seizure in which someone may fall to the ground, go still for a few seconds, then start twitching. This part of the seizure may last a few minutes, then be followed by a long sleep. A tonic-clonic seizure is also sometimes called a "grand mal," which is French for "big illness."

torso The middle part of your body, from your neck to the tops of your legs.

trigger Something that sets off a seizure. Two common triggers of epilepsy are tiredness and hunger.

Useful organizations

HERE ARE SOME ORGANIZATIONS YOU MIGHT LIKE TO CONTACT FOR
MORE INFORMATION ABOUT EPILEPSY

EPILEPSY FOUNDATION OF AMERICA
5351 Garden City Drive
Landover, MD 20785-7223
Tel: 0113 2108800
Works for children and adults affected by seizures.

THE EPILEPSY INSTITUTE
257 Park Ave. South
New York, NY 10010
www.epilepsyinstitute.org
Provides information about epilepsy and tries to improve quality of life for epileptics and their families.

**CITIZENS UNITED FOR RESEARCH IN EPILEPSY
(CURE)**
505 North Lake Shore Drive
Chicago, IL 60611
www.cureepilepsy.org
Raises public awareness and supports research to find a cure.

OTHER WEBSITES

www.epilepsy.org.uk/kids/index/html
Provides stories, games and a gallery for children (from the British Epilepsy Association).

www.eyie.org
Gives young people an opportunity of discussing epilepsy and its effect on their lives.

www.ibe-epilepsy.org
Provides international news and activities for people with epilepsy.

www.efa.org/
Provides a site for teenagers, where they can play games or meet other young people with epilepsy, plus links to related sites.

Index